World within the World

Poems / Prose Poems

Sam Rasnake

in memory of my Mother, W. Gray Rasnake
mmhh-mmhh

for Mary

Works by Sam Rasnake

Necessary Motions

Lessons in Morphology

Tales of Brave Ulysses (Poetry Series)

Religions of the Blood

Inside a Broken Clock

Cinéma Vérité

World within the World

Contents

I Groanings Under the Eaves

II Ambiguities of Dark and Light

III Every Moment Is a Window

When you take a flower in your hand and really look at it,

it's your world for the moment.

– Georgia O'Keeffe

The world about us would be desolate

except for the world within us.

– Wallace Stevens

I

Groanings Under the Eaves

An Empty Easel, an Opened Window, a Paint Box on Hardwood Floor

And if my words were a painting, the colors could explain
the story, then you would see the connections and say yes,
I see the connections between light and shadow, all textures
of what was meant or believed to be. What a clever thing,
you might say. How different from everything else. How
lucky. But if the words were shades only – What then?
A dozen shades to explain all the baggage depth carries
with it: the stone floor, perfumed water, lounging couch,
mahogany trim, a shoulder, a thigh, a foot – the raised dots,
showing only the determined press of an experienced hand,
are nothing by themselves, but together show a real life,
entirely. The eyes are too compelling, in fact, you won't be
able to break away. Your neck, your legs, your fingers
locked in place where you stand, a fix of wonder and dread.
And if words were brush, my thoughts with one stroke
would smear off into a perfect blend of satisfactions. If
words were canvas centered on an empty wall, the stories,
complete with flashback, flash-forward, and twist of plot,
might be told. And if the words were wall? – I would
hold the roof of you to stillness, a bank of clouds overhead
swathing the stars into their silent and darkest cold.

The Body Is What I Say It Is

– a geometry of Picasso's Les Demoiselles d'Avignon, *1907*

The products of time never finish.
There is no innocence lost.
Dark streets, collar turned to the wind,

then lit rooms of hands and breasts,
of sheets wrapped in thighs, and feet
with fruit on the floor. The absolute

freedom of the mask, of the body's
blue and red abandon – in a world,
such a necessary and ugly place,

we've never learned to see. Outside,
the war whispers, and electricity,
like a drunken skull, waits her turn.

World within the World

Huang Chen-hsiao, Gathering at the
Orchard Pavilion, *carved ivory,*
3 5/8" x 1 5/8" (1739)

Only the most delicate
of fingers would attempt
to bring the lives of trees
from ivory – the elephant
forgotten, and shelter
not the point – the path
as purpose, the clarity –
along the way there will be
a moment to speak, to give
yourself to nothing,
to know that your feet
in motion is the point

Notes for a Life. In a Swing.
No Wind to Speak of.

– *Sally Mann,* Untitled (Deep South #23), *1998*

The field is the mouth of the dead.
Starlings drift the summer's late amber
as though a photograph's gelatin silver

has come to life, and you breathe in,
you breathe out – that other world.
Your lungs are sadness, full-measured.

A perfect moment. The scarred tree's
gift is silence. At the edge of hearing,
the slow river's story – all moss and

bush – slips its bridge between darkness
and darkness – while the sky, always
the patient *doppelgänger,* sits on water.

Whole forests & towns & time swallowed
in ivy. One trickle of sweat beside the ear.
Somewhere a banjo, somewhere a hound.

Solitudes as Meditation

– after Edward Hopper

1. A House

It must be morning.
Long bellies of cloud hug
such a thin edge of ground
there's no way of knowing
what world the road bends to –
uncut grass, browned deep,
an after-thought of scattered pines,
this house with blinds in place
behind dark windows. Someone
still comes here, still knows.
A creak here, a scratch there,
wind at the chimney's mouth,
then groaning under the eaves.

2. A Room

A woman sits on the bed –
all verities of a life half-lived
become the light on her feet,
an aching of crossed arms,
wordless shadows of a story
her eyes fall to. The hard city
looms at both stifling windows
for balance, hers and the painter's
– his hand a motion of grief that
finds its form in the lover's body,
facedown in an ignorant pillow.

3. *Night Journeys*

The luggage is packed for
comings or leavings that blur
to silence. Only a dark square
of window near the room's
bright, fevered edge gives
hope against the will's deepest
appetite that settles onto the page,
two knees, and the unused bed –
a letter whose truth must dull
the body – its shoulders and
thin shadows, sagging toward
the fingers of disbelief.

My Last Door

Very green out the window
A most perfect mountain
And light on the river
                is particular in its leaving
The world is still
                but somewhere, a persistent
mockingbird...
I have come to the end of something

      – from her letters, Georgia O'Keeffe

Lie down on this table
and life is believable

Stars are easy

Deep curls of limbs ready
a night so tall the world
stands on its head

————————————

Your tongue is warm
Your words intent on defining
the motion that isn't needed
when blue is enough
and your fingers are hidden

————————————

My mouth is a leaf
My hair drifts to sea
but I leave the words of a fool
on the bank of this book's dark folds

————————————

I try to stay away from the flowers
but the deep hints of your red won't let me go

After an hour of watching
I melt and pool against the hard floor

then you daub me to your brush
so the fine hairs can work me into shadow

————————————

The hot sky goes on –
past every limit

You walk from here

————————————

A dark fall waters the arroyo –
black bolt – cuts the earth
down to my toes

I feel the shaking

The Sleep of Trees, Three Parables

– after paintings by F. Scott Hess

The Measure of Love

When is a glass of water only a glass of water? And nothing
more. No attachments to anything. Some questions, after all,
have no answers, and this might be one of them.

Tight bands of umber, coral, and grey filter through rafters
of the unfinished room. Lights in the valley begin to sprinkle
on. It's all about scale. The dance – unnoticed, undisturbed
– carries its motion of faces into wood and glass and paint.
Call it family. All the tools of the heart and hand, of the eye
and ear are in place.

We nail together the days for shelter against the cold. We
believe in a measure for pain. On a scale of 0-10, a doctor
says, where is your pain? How does it feel? At the end, a
number is nothing more than number.

So, when is the glass only a glass, and water, only water?
When is my life only my life? I set down the glass and pour
it full. A couple of drops splashing against the table as I pick
it up, then take a long drink.

There's a soft wind in the dust of trees. And hands at work –
building, building. The night is coming on with its slender
threads of knowing.

The Sleep of Trees

There are storms in the memory of sleep.
What I remember though is not what happened.
What happened was more than enough.
And through the opened window, what the trees had to
        say was the rest of my life.
My life then was the light that creeps in back of a storm,
        the light against the downpour, against the shake of
        thunder. I pace window to window, room to room –
        a flood always in my thoughts.
Maybe every sleep carries its own storm.
Maybe every sleep waits like a kindness never given though
        felt as if everything depended on its smallest word.
        Waits for the next morning. And the next.

Riverbed

All I can tell you of trees is this: They grew in the riverbed – the scrub and bush and occasional tree – outside the city, though this was no real river – just a bed for runoff. But there was a flood. There must have been. And it washed me here – some little death, some fetal curl among the spindly limbs. Shoes, missing. My legs bent, my wrinkled nightgown, my eyes opened to a heavy sky, and away from the one who watches me. Or, does he sleep too? I couldn't say. But with such a quiet bending of the wrist, my left hand edges closer to him.

*

He has no idea how long he's been coming here, day after day, to this spot, curling beneath the dead woman in her tree. Just to look. Some days he's sure he sees her move, other times, no. She doesn't move, hasn't moved. He can't help himself. He doesn't know why he's not wearing any shoes or socks, doesn't know where he's left them. Sometimes he almost thinks of it, but never does. Not knowing is good. It makes him happy. Too afraid to laugh out loud, he chuckles to his mouth, grinds his teeth to silence. Show respect, he thinks. One day – though not today – I'll touch her hand. Near his feet, in a puddle of water, the butterfly rests on a stone.

The Artist Alone

– Francesca Woodman, Self-deceit, *Rome, 1978-1979*

She crawls a maze of cold and damp to the very edge of familiar. All truth is blurred. Leaning against the wall, the mirror, more in place than out, is how she looks at her real hand – if those are the best words – as if she doesn't remember why she's come – all sinew and shade, soft curve of the hip, a bit done for – or why her hand has lived its life and she has lived hers, lost in the hard ruins, unwilling to stop until she disappears into that other Rome, slick with rain and more time than could ever be needed.

These walls are no match for her. She hides because there's nothing left. She turns away her face, her motion a haze to silence, her breath a fragile wing of air.

A Corridor in the Asylum

*– Vincent van Gogh, painting, oil color and
gouache on pink Ingres paper,
Saint-Paul-de-Mausole in St. Rémy,
September 1889*

Walls are closing in,
quick-funnel
to stillness,

and the figure,
rejected priest of a man
who's left his god
in a room

he's long since forgotten
opens each door,

pale light leaking
over his face in hosannas
no god could bear
to hear, but

there's nothing
anxious in his body,
browned numb
with acceptance,

with the walking,
nothing glutted,

no want – only paint,

a tremor
over dried brush hairs
to awkward silence

Delay in Glass

No obstinacy, ad absurdum, of hiding
the coition through a glass pane
*   – Marcel Duchamp*

There are no tapestries here,
no weaving, no nights spent
undoing empires worth saving

We are glass & tubes & gears
that grind the wheels that turn
under a metal veil streaming

as if a single life – forgotten or
remembered – could be forged
in blasts of sand and steel

For the Reader, Turning Pages in a Book, Happy Thanksgiving

– Goya, Los Desastres de la Guerra, *1810-1820*

In the etchings of loss and war by Goya
there's not one contented moment, no
pause, no burst of satisfaction. And you,
seated at your safe table in a well-lit room,
food in the oven, people coming over,
the talk and laughter, "Hi, how are you –"
thousands of miles and scores of years
from any truth – no wish you were here
in these settings. Impossible to envy
the art or the artist, to love the very human
body of his hand. The rape, the stolen clothes,
and wasted fields. An admiration of the dead
on the happy face glutted with a job well done.
The world is a plague but is what you were born for.

Sonnet Vortex

At the print gallery we weave together all dislocated thoughts –
a plumber's snake, bowls for ketchup, aquarium bubble, electric
bill – into one happy word at the print gallery we assemble
everything you need – the wall, chair, bedpost, website, unopened
petroleum jelly, as many stone coasters as cups – missing no parts,
leaving out nothing to forget when we're done, we guarantee all
work at the print gallery your satisfaction comes first then we –
such an important symbol for the planet, for space, for nebulae of
any kindness ever completed at this gallery the presses never stop
their breathing or wheeze in the clank of metal against idea,
spitting out, near the end, the finished product of a young man's
gaze at the painting of a ship in a harbor in a town in a house in
a cupola in a hallway in a painting of himself and the ship in a
harbor town in the house in a cupola in the hallway *What I give*
    form to in daylight is only one percent of what I have
    seen in darkness –
    MC Escher

II

Ambiguities of Dark and Light

Learning the Patience of Stones

– for Joy Harjo, after reading Secrets from
the Center of the World

If you wait long enough, the sky becomes crow,
and her deep song, the one the mockingbird hates,
is a song you know already, have always known,
but were afraid to sing –

                    afraid the words would fail you
or wouldn't choose your tongue – afraid you would fail
the words and a thousand winters of truth would rage
against your shoulders until silence was the only voice –
afraid to know something, afraid to do or be,
afraid to remember … to forget.

                    Can you see that hill?
that river with its smoothed rocks buried deep
in the going? moss along its edges? the stand of pines
much older than words?

                    Here, the mountains are stone
upon stone. They know the patience of waiting.
They know how to be still,
and move.

Mountain Verse

– a photograph, Backbone Rock, Holston Mountain, 2004

Someone tried to build a fence here,
a line that says there is always the *other*.
The one post is dislodged.

Under stands
of pine & spruce & chestnut, water pours
from some dark certainty of earth
with deep smells of myth in its belly,

spills
down the ridge a soaked quilt of stones,
smooth and moss-covered.

Past rusted wire
that spans the creek, mountain laurels lift
hosanna from the cool tangles of green and brown,
empty their bodies to this holiness, into a dust of sky
that settles its waiting down steep walls of blue,
as perfect an afternoon as can be lived.

Starting with Rodin's *The Walking Man*

to write the self into poetry,
to build a life, line by line,
into face & hands & shoulders
we recognize, or at least convince
ourselves we know, into an arm
that points across the winter river,
a foot that must ache, a cloud
of breath for speech, a penis sagging
with the cold, then from the page
this body stands – its thighs swollen,
its knees bent, eyes scanning the slow,
deliberate world – its tiny arc of myth
and grief dwarfed against the maw
of nothing – and learns to walk

For the Painter's Hand

– Henri Matisse, Blue Nude, *1907*

Forget the poet's view of woman's hips
as more than moon, her mouth as more
than sun – For your hand, her hips are
the earth and have the perfect shape
to still your eyes. Forget the moon.
It's the soil you crave in your fingers,
it's the ache for rain – her mouth that's
all tease. You'd be willing to die there,
her tongue flicking vowels in a snag
of e's and o's. Her thighs, her belly
and arm – a contrapposto of smoke
and shade. You feel her – throbbing
in both temples, a bleed of color
and light over canvas. The scrape
of brush, your only voice.

The Pleasure's in the Doing

Katsushika Hokusai, Kajikazawa
in Kai Province, *woodblock,*
c. 1830-1834

As if stirring from sleep,
thick banks of mist wade
the mountain's easy slope.
Only the peak is real.
Here, an arm of green
cliff over the wave's
blue cold, and four lines
down into a wash of caps.
Back bent with the current
as though retelling a story
to the wind, the fisherman
waits the tug at his hard
but patient hand. Something
dark slips away into silence,
something beautiful opens
its terrible jaws.

Love Poem with Eyebrow

– Frida Kahlo, Self-Portrait, *1940*

Like any woman, deep rivers
of passion meet between her eyes.
At the point where the hairs touch,
hot rivers, heated by a patient sleep,

will wait, if need be, for as long
as it takes this jungle to become
our familiar country. She bleeds
from thorns that cut her neck.

The necklace is broken. A dead hummingbird
will bring her luck, bring her love.
Bright curves of flowers become dragonflies,
butterflies, a brooch to wear. Maybe

she's a warrior, a sweet Christ
who dies an uncommon lover.
Her spider monkey won't pray with her,
too busy thinking. But the cat

survives – haunches down behind
her shoulder – against the wall of leaves,
full-veined, that carry life
into some strong, forgotten place.

Sketches, a *Study for Three Heads*, 1962

– after Francis Bacon

First, let me say I'm not thinking. I haven't thought for
days now, and it's easy to do – or rather, not to. Here's
the trick – take a nail and hammer, placing the sharp point
against the belly of any thought, then bang away until
the nail head disappears into skull wall. I do this again
and again until no thought remains, until emptiness is
the story's refusal to end.

My jaws are swollen.

Why three heads, you ask? Three is a perfect number.
As in godhead, trinity, trilogy, threesome, ménage à trois.
Triplet, triptych, tribunal. A triangle, a third world trio,
third party, the first odd prime, the basic unit of matter,
one three-dollar bill. Three as in stages: birth living death.
Lithium, magi, musketeers. The Larry, Moe, & Curly spin.
Three as in axis, allies, or blt. Three things to tell you:
loss, loss, and more loss.

The faces dissolve. The sexes dissolve to *he she hot cold*
as if the moment drips away in my hand's blast of heat,
in my brush's perfect ease to hard truth – its one kindness.

I drink too much for even the thinnest breath of clarity –
such a desperate stretch of what to know.

Man of Sorrows

– after the marble statue by
Marion Perkins, 1950

One who has known all too well
how marble surrenders to the slow
grief of chisel to hammer – how it
breaks away, bit by bit, until truth
finds its shape, its crease of hurt
and purpose – one who could in fact
walk on water if need be or the lost
and deserted streets of Jackson,
Birmingham, Chicago – one who
has the heavy, shut eyes and pursed
lips of a 1950's would-be perfect
world of soda fountain and stool, its
open collars, canvas sneakers, and
the hard fist of absolute refusal

To Paint

No. 18 *(1948), Mark Rothko*

> *I don't express myself in painting.*
> *I express my not-self. – MR*

Start with unholy terrors in dabs
of orange & ochre & blue. Learn
to multiform the vain tragedies of
a waking life –

      with wicked smiles,
all toothy and impossible to resist –
in blocks, empty of myth, symbol
or place.

      Let go your name to razor
and pill. Who could miss such a thing?
It's science run amuck. Find a window
to the fevered world –

      a starless edge,
an end of nothing to nothing still.

What Is Unsaid

– after the painting by Judith Peck,
2019, oil on board

The eyes drop
in a search for
change or purpose

or loveliness of
the skin his other
world cannot see

or will not as if
there's no way
to go on from

here (a wound so
bottomless) unless
this is spoken

aloud at least
or the moment
opens – but

I am projecting
onto instead of
gleaning from

as if we find our
selves in lines of
paint – in what is

– or maybe in some
thing out of view
that whispers

another story and
another still until
there is no difference

Scrolling

*Nothing is absolute. Everything changes, everything moves,
everything revolves, everything flies and goes away.*
                                    – Frida Kahlo

1. Languages of / in the Body

   *– Nude Male Drawings 12, 22, & 9,
         Gordon Punt, 2011-2012*

*this   this world   no color
must be   to what*
                    [false start]

To what world of no
color does he give his
body with its hidden

need for raw edges
for the push and push
into the rippled life:

a blistered haiku
must show everything
but its name

2. *Dialogue with Impression*

> – Closer, Touch, Impression, *hyperreal drawings,*
> *Paul Cadden, c. 2011*

The mouth is a perfect
invitation but what of
the in and out of water
pushing against some
unseen grief she carries
in her body –
>   *all those*
years of silences when
the talking is not talking –
of desperate longings
when the having is not
having –
>   pushing as if
youth were the giving
up or the giving in –

the beauty of always
moving closer and closer
still but never finding
until distance is the truth
of never –
>   pencil moving
over recycled paper making
a perfect moment of what is not

3. Looking Back

> – Notes in Time, The First Language, *and* Torture
>   of Women *by Nancy Spero, 1979, 1981, 1975-1976*

In the history of pain and electric shocks among the voices
that matter and do not I am the corpse of the state I am
the state of daughter of mother of sister of giving of victim
I am the other the one breathing in the world I did and
did not make I am   the one   speaking unheard the one
listening unasked I am the one in the history of first things

the language of voices moving the body the mounds of
paper dolls of prison of freedom the hardest of truths I do
and do not dance as if I am the story itself the hot spheres
crossing dark banks of nothing of stars as guidepost with
their own truths to tell I am waiting   o   I am waiting
in the history of this thing I am waiting in this poem these

words   these spaces   these hollowed out eyes gazing
the sounds of the tongue I am the one moving space
into words against teeth I am the sharp point the saying
and the said in the history of pain I am the hidden gift
the dark and beautiful of a history I did not write but am
I am dancing off this page into the whole into never

Aimless

A photograph is a secret about a secret.
The more it tells you, the less you know.
– Diane Arbus

Still Life with Table for Disconnection

Take this family, on their lawn one Sunday in Westchester, NY,
a sea of grey for green. The best way for me to show you how
it feels or doesn't feel to be unable, unwilling to find the self
in the backyard. A littered study of 1968 Americana. We hide

our faces as if no one will notice, soak up the perfect oblivion
of want – table for disconnection, towel for covering the sacred.
So this is worship – our bodies, a temple of dream. The trees
never stop their haunting. The sun burns through whatever

this love is or isn't, down to the soul's quick, polished, then
emptied for this moment of suburbia we close our eyes to.
The long gaze into a child's plastic wading pool. And five
decades later, we ghost the silence of an *is* becoming a *was*

without our knowing how. Maybe things don't just happen.
The sliver of space between having and lost is razor thin.

It

>   *– NYC, 1962*

Penelope Tree in her living room looks
more "whiter shade of pale" than "love
me do," more question than answer. Her
arms crossed with an edge of anger, feet
planted against the hard truth of happy,
an absolute resolve creased between her
eyes. Her life is not her own is the best
way to tell it – the daily rituals of the
flowered vase, plush rugs for looks only,
embroidered pillows, thick curtains for
secrets. But she will find it. Everything
gives way in time to tremors of youth in
her body – a body so set, so sure of itself
uncertainty is the only possible end
which is beauty's point in the first place.

A Parable

– Jorge Luis Borges, Central Park, 1969

An old man's stubby fingers, hands crossed
in front, resting on a cane – his dark suit a simile
for loss, the hard face, a chiseled study of wind,
of time. From his brain's deep well, he draws

a wearied grief – the exotic bits of *I* he stuffs
in his pockets. Over both shoulders the winter trees
stretch their bent spines into a stiff, sleeping sky.
His words are mirrors, incapable of telling what

they know. Blindness is his anodyne for terrors of
the heart, for questions with no answers, for ambiguities
of dark and light. A head with a hole. This room with
no door. And the mantra? *To live without needing.*

Self-Portrait, Pregnant, N.Y.C., 1945

Darkness holds in
its sex for and by
and with and to,
then rubs its edges
smooth, its dreams
of surrender to the
whisper, to the well-
placed hand, a mouth
screwed to its rawest
possibility: the belly
swollen with forever –
such terrible beauty,
this ache for such
ugly perfection

Acceptance Must Be the Highest Art

– A Woman with her baby monkey, N.J., 1971

The strongest look – or is it unshakable
love – between Mother and child is not
a fractured gaze into the black hollows
of each other's eyes (no room for ego
or reason) but in the same direction,
out and beyond, into the sacred *what
if*, where dreams hide their one gift in
storms of the nothing that must be
something though we have no words,
no labels for it, no way of telling any
version, as if that were needed or better
or even possible. This look doesn't care
about that. It only knows, only wants
the truth of holding and being held.

III

Every Moment Is a Window

Woman in Mask

Love in war time must be like this: eyes as moons,
tracking their smoothed arcs around all wrecks fused
to one. She swims, if that is the word, great swirls

of teal, mustard, and envy in the hard *kkhhlluugg*
of her breathing until only the silence remains.
Her mask, a desperate gift to fingers, is like

that one perfect moment in a B movie when
the woman, refusing to be victim, rises from a cold,
misted lake, the terrible and beautiful dripping

from her body – she stumbles to a shore, long since
willed to nothing, then disappears into some murky,
relentless gnarl of trees for absolute reckoning.

*– after a painting by Alex Russell Flint, cover
art for Poets / Artists, #42, Jan. 2013*

An Urban Meditation

Make a model of a good life
– quotation by Kiki Smith

Cold and grizzled flecks of
snow on the fouled stoop
clean the world or at
least this city of its
night, of its death
in life in art as if
the only myth
were Lilith's
glass eyes
of truth
turned
to mine

A Picture's Worth

a 1,000 looks I never saw
This must have been
a good year Wish I could
remember

The eyes say beauty is
in the heavy silence And
the mirror my accomplice
my telling

What I carry to the grave
You can be so busy creating
it becomes your only
living No

future only past A pawn of
thin shadows for a life without
certainty You have no
final say

— *Vivian Maier,* Self-Portrait, 1955

sur·veil·lance

\sər-ˈvā-lən(t)s *also* -ˈvāl-yən(t)s *or* -ˈvā-ən(t)s\

Noun: the act of carefully watching someone or something especially
in order to prevent or detect a crime; close watch kept over
someone or something

Origin: French, from *surveiller* to watch over, from *sur-* +*veiller* to
watch, from Old French *veillier,* from Latin *vigilare, from
vigil* watchful –

First Known Use: 1802

– Merriam-Webster

This is the how to: an end of starting the middle with all pleasures [or
here you may want to insert your own dynamic] *pleasures made real*
as in fragments of faces in smears of time, in a river of lights, both
white and red, in the dark whir of highways. That is all you'll need to
give over your irresistible life to the wish and grind [feel free to insert
music as soundtrack, maybe "Feeling so Real" or "Long Snake Moan"].
Someone always knows. Someone watches your doings and undoings
[taking notes, naming names, knocking down doors, shooting photos
through zoom lenses to animate the whatever into stacks of evidence
for crimes yet to be determined]. The camera is unconcerned with any
difference between *doesn't care your ups or downs, your gift among
thieves* and *any wherewithal or hitherto of a night gone voyeur.*
Then, there is the *look* – as if to name *it* is self-gratification of the
hidden kind, or – if learning is your bent – to call it *truth in language*
meant to save you/us, meant to give us/you anything but believing [and

this is what you write once you realize you're repeating yourself]
believing in an archive [one that's kept in some immaculate and fool-
proof safe – such an improbability given the fact we're all fools wearing
our techno-motleys of a tweet here & a post there or a facetime as
substitute for flesh (but where was I? Oh yes) – *fool-proof safe* in
some underground bunker – expansive, windowless, and climate-
controlled – maintained by as many pocket-protectors as Big Brother
Big Sister requires] knowing all the while that anything but truth will do.
One eye watches – "We see you," it says – while the other sleeps, and
we're happy, or think ourselves to be, so we keep watching, we keep
breathing – *mmmmmm* – and the highways whir until we stop ourselves
from stopping, as in snakes – eating our own tails – no hands, no legs,
like nesting dolls – down to a single silence – our only dream for change.

– after Surveillance, *photograph by Julie Dunham*

I Always Knew

– Contact Sheet, Candy Darling, by Peter Hujar

The fierce, lonely pillow of silence in
the Columbia University Medical Center,
that early Spring of '74, had no way of

knowing then the beauty in its deepest crease.
The heart only wants what it believes, only
believes what it knows, only knows what it feels.

There never was enough time or place or show
to tell the truth as it should have been. She was
waiting for the man. Outside the window, down

the darkness, around the hard edges – all streets
were perfection. Even then, there was only *then*.
There was no call. There was no word for it.

A Book of Judith

1. Surprise and Menace

– Judith Beheading Holofernes, *Caravaggio, 1598*

On the English students' lounge wall,
the moment of steel and a man's throat
make the taut threads of blood like stiff
lines for big game fish shoot away from
his eyes and opened mouth that search,
in vain of course, for some bit, some root
to grab hold of – his hand fisted with
the rumpled sheet while she and she
standing by the bed, the look of strange
naiveté or threat on both their faces –
impossible to say which in this light or
time – meanwhile, a dark red, the future
maybe, shoulders over them, topping off
the painting with its perfect gift of doubt

2. Artemisia at Her Canvas

– during or just after the trial of Agostino Tassi, 1612

After *Judith Slaying Holofernes*,
a flawless symmetry of blind pursuit
that even Caravaggio couldn't get at
with his paints, this darker vengeance
that would never rest in the sacred
or profane, did find its own truth, its
mound of flesh in full measures of rage
by her determined hand – his head
slipping free of its stubborn shoulders,
no worries of kingdom then, of lies or
damaged goods, to twisted bedsheet
in great spurts of blood, then a slow
and beautiful silence, such sweet
payback for art's willful grieving

3. Archetypes of Will

> – *Rembrandt,* Judith Beheading Holofernes,
>   pen drawing, c.1653

These deliberate
    truths of ink on
paper remove all
    doubt from her
eyes – and here is
    the deed: such
a deep and final
    cut while sleeping,
– even warriors must
    have their dreaming –
both hands clear in
    their devising as if
to say that time will
    never be enough

4. Deconstructing the Femme Fatale

   – Judith and Holofernes II, *Franz von Stuck, c. 1927*

So now this: the unexpected thrill of shadow,
of blue on red – a fire burning, its shimmers
to submission meant to last, meant to carry
no regret, and there is none.

                         No breath of
grief in the dark pleasures of meat and wine,
not in seduction's sweetest touch to the tongue.
Something to control, something to call
your own.

     Nothing hidden. And her look is
the perfect moment – a tilt of the head the gods
would surely understand, her hands to steel.

His body sleeping, both hands curled open –
in the silent, blinded will of a generation,
having everything to do with power –
And love? Only paint drying on canvas.

5. Departures Into / Out of

> – Judith with the Head of Holofernes,
> *Elisa Johns, 2010*

There's no orgasm in this story. I'm through
with myth, she must think by this time. Blood,
berry, and pomegranate juice pool their way
out of the painting. Her pumps and chair – very
vogue – her gown and nails complete the look.
Such a finished, hard stare. Tired of the hunt,
tired of empire. White is its own defiance.
How much of the personal does it take anyway?

In the basket by her feet, his head, eyes closed,
as though waiting – not for retribution, not pride,
not hot pleasures of the body to die for – is done
with the taking, is all about the *otherness*. Now,
the world is a small window of blue to grey to
black, an occasional bird, great swirls of cloud.

Always Comes in Threes

Myths are public dreams, dreams are private myths.
*   – Joseph Campbell*

[Studies in Leda]

Leda Revisited

*   – after Jesús Helguera, Cy Twombly, Perri Neri*

a time when all resistance to
the forbidden is let go, when
there's nothing but need – no I,

no you – when the delirious
fumblings of the body find
their rhythms in splatters

of truth and impossibility – no
matter if someone watches,
every moment is a window

Sketches

     – after Gustav Klimt, Man Ray, Betty Dodson

so we sketch history to paper
and what body wouldn't surrender
to the gods knowing the pleasure

that would come – what body
wouldn't crave the most hidden
places of the brain – the one joy,

irresistible in its taste and touch,
the one moment in flesh when myth
shivers silence to everything new

Body to Body

> *– after Bartolomeo Ammannati, Reuben Nakian,*
> *Fernando Botero*

"obsessive by nature like the body" is
how, in sleep, the body mirrors itself
– what it wants, aches for, demands –

and in *that* sleep finds a perfect scream,
a passion, the release of its own will,
finds the dark and wonderful – like

the speed of light from brain to nerve
ending to touch – the one thing never
seen, never tongued to words:

Standing Figure

– Henry Moore, 1950

The human head has been
replaced. All knots and stems,

a disembodied thing from its
rocky plinth stares over the dark

Scottish landscape, an obsession
with nothingness a few would say –
in truth, a sheep farm. Two eye-like

spheres, little humans or refugees
from some interior life, extend

their long and slender necks into
this cold, forbidding place –

A Fragment, with Mask and Horn

– after a drawing by Cheryl Dodds

There were obsessions. Mine and yours.
Distractions really. Life getting in the way of life.
Yours was brush or pencil or camera, with swirls

of black and grey on walls of white. No time for
a splash of color. And mine? A word, a space,

a voice. Like Borges thinking of Borges – knowing
a truth, with its grinding bent on horizons of
undoing, but no map for charting there to here.

The mask holds the sea in its hard grooves,
looks on, while the dancer wakes the primal need
of take on take, in a twist of brass and spit,
in a dream of flesh with its poundings
of sweat, of desire, in a breath
that's more than wild.

Silence in Charcoal

– after Brian David Martin, Utterance
(charcoal on paper)

The charcoaled stillness
of the dark grows thick,
but there are no words
for this – only shadows
and the one light as cold
reminders to the room that
the black window forgives
the overturned table its why
and how for mocking the chair.
There must have been voices,
strained or unwilling, but those
rattles over the pallid kitchen floor
have vanished into night's hard and
silent grains outside the cool glass where
another story with its meager sift, its flash
of disconnection for the restless eye, wields
such a desperate plot, and what is seen through
the closed window at night is always vulnerable,
singular, exact – lesson from Baudelaire. No bodies,
no touch, no moving – just a long and willful silence.

What We Do Most of All

– after The Walk to Paradise *Garden,*
W. Eugene Smith, 1946

The children have no idea
of the science of hate or
the earth's deep sex wound,
all the generations with flesh
burned to skull, their legs and
arms gone, nipple and genital.
Eyes, mouth, ears – gone.
The universe must tremble
above this fruited plain
though it doesn't show
in the photograph. This is
the silence of *after*. This is
the gathering of pieces.
One child leads the other,
looks off slightly to the right
into deep wood as he walks.
The one who follows gives
no thought to where she's going.
Her look is straight ahead.
I can't say what gilded light
or blinding path it is
that swallows them both,
that leaves nothing but
shadow prints to say
they were ever even there.

Art Lessons from Jung's Notebook of Dreams

(an unfinished manuscript, the Lake of Zurich, 1960)

Sometimes it just happens. It's the moment, the mood, the end.
    Pouring coffee into a sink, leaving the appearance of one
    perfect note, a sixteenth, beside the drain.

This, I think, can be explained by Kandinsky: everything
    that's dead quivers.

*

Find the genesis.

The disturbing object is the first step: shaman with horns & hoofs,
    stone alignment at Carnac, sticks of the *I Ching*, a debased
    god, his golden shower on the essential female, and Picasso
    conceives a war.

*

Consider Hieronymus Bosch, painting himself into his *Garden
    of Delights*, wet hairs of the brush finding absolute instinct
    in his hand, or consider *Garden of Delights* finished,
    those bestial knots of humanity searching for a point.

And the religion for *this* hundred years (italics mine)? Max Ernst
    scratches his own enigma on granite boulders of the Forno
    glacier. This one I call *unus mundus*.

A four-eyed anima.
Still Life with Vase of Nasturtiums.
Sketches of a human head, LSD-25, Germany, *circa* 1951.

One meaning leads to the next, etc. Like a black square, finally,
    on a white ground. Discordant harmonics, a grieving
    world, one mustard seed. Cornell's *Pavillion.* Nakian's *Rape
    of Lucrece.*

*

Learn to disregard all marginalia. Surely Leonardo's drawing of
    a human heart is not so cold as to allow us to forget
    the real body, unseen, holding in its dark cavity this muscle.

*

In *Limits of Understanding*, Paul Klee's lines & ladders & shade
    fill two-thirds of the field, try to open another dimension
    (out of and into) but are useless. It's the circle that depicts,
    with a rather dark precision, what, in fact, cannot be known.
    What is felt, I must add, is outside the painting, the hand,
    outside the thinned cap of skull.

*

Schwitters for a decade works with garbage (cathedrals built for
    things not people) & Miro collects at dawn what the sea
    washes up. There is the sea. There's Pollock, possessed,
    dripping paint over canvas, dead at 44 & Chagall's lonely
    blue man, hovering & Arp (one I can follow) with his
    Leaves arranged according to the laws of chance.

*

Suddenly, the collapse of the atom makes sense, and is, so to
speak, a comfort.

*

After Hiroshima the style is panic shown in the body, is thinking
the unsayable.

After Breton an idiot is any man who cannot see horses galloping
along an edge of tomato.

After the tomato, nothing.

Notes

"Solitudes as Meditation," pp.14-16: The individual poems in this suite are based on paintings by Edward Hopper: "A House" / *Solitude*, 1944; "A Room" / *Summer in the City*, 1950; "Night Journeys" / *Hotel Room*, 1931.

"My Last Door," pp.17-18: In addition to the poem's title being the same as a painting, 1952-1954, by Georgia O'Keeffe, other works by her lend description throughout the lines.

"The Sleep of Trees, Three Parables," pp.19-21: The titles of the individual sections of the prose poem are, correspondingly, the titles of the paintings by F. Scott Hess: *The Measure of Love*, 2004; *The Sleep of Trees*, 2000; *Riverbed*, 2004.

"Delay in Glass," p.25: Marcel Duchamp's *The Bride Stripped Bare by Her Bachelors, Even*, 1915-1923 (9 feet tall and freestanding, two panes of glass with materials such as lead foil, fuse wire, and dust) is the basis for this poem.

"Sonnet Vortex," p.27: The poem is based on *Print Gallery*, 1956, (lithograph) by M.C. Escher.

"Learning the Patience of Stones," p.30: *Secrets from the Center of the World*, mentioned in the epigraph, is a collaborative book with text by Joy Harjo and photographs by Stephen Strom.

"Starting with Rodin's *The Walking Man*," p.32: Auguste Rodin's *The Walking Man*, c. 1877, 1907 (bronze, cast by Fonderie Alexis Rudier, 1913) is the inspiration for this poem.

"What Is Unsaid," pp.39-40: Of the poem, the artist Judith Peck wrote: "This is exactly what I was feeling painting this piece. If I could write with my soul this is what I would have said."

"Scrolling," p.43: In "Looking Back," the works by Nancy Spero referenced are *Notes in Time*, 1979 (cut-and-pasted painted paper, gouache, and pencil on joined sheets of paper); *The First Language*, 1981 (cut-and-pasted collage, hand printing, painting on paper, 22 panels); *Torture of Women*, 1975-1976 (collage of juxtaposed image and text, hand-printed and typewritten words, 14 panels, 125 feet in length).

"Aimless," pp.44-45: All sections are based on photographs by Diane Arbus and are marked either by titles or in epigraphs except "Still Life with Table for Disconnection" / *A Family on their lawn one Sunday in Westchester, New York*, 1968 and "It" / *Penelope Tree in her living room, NYC*, 1962.

"A Picture's Worth," p.52: Vivien Maier, working primarily as a nanny in Chicago and New York City, took thousands of photos, many of them self-portraits. Her primary subjects, other than herself, were children, the elderly, and those marginalized by society. Of the more than 120,000 negatives she left behind when she died in 2009, only 4,000 were printed. Around two thousand undeveloped rolls of film were also discovered.

"I Always Knew," p.55: When Candy Darling – actress, underground superstar of The Factory (Andy Warhol's art studio in New York City), and transgender icon – was hospitalized in October 1973, she asked Peter Hujar to photograph her in the hospital bed. Hujar's contact sheets contain 60 images – the last ever taken of Darling. She died of lymphoma in 1974 at the age of 29.

"A Book of Judith," p.57: "Artemisia at Her Canvas" is based on *Judith Slaying Holofernes*, a painting completed by Artemisia Gentileschi in 1613. In 1612, Agostino Tassi was convicted of raping Artemisia. The violence against her, her public testimony during Tassi's seven-month trial, and her rapist's conviction, no doubt, influenced the painting.

"Always Comes in Threes," pp.61-63: "Leda Revisited" is based on Jesús Helguera, *Leda y el Cisne*, 1947 (oil on canvas); Cy Twombly, *Leda and the Swan*, 1962 (pencil, crayon, oil paint); Perri Neri, *Leda and the Swan*, 2015 (oil on canvas and magazine pages). | "Sketches" is based on Gustav Klimt, *Semi-Nude leaning forward*, 1913-1914 (pencil, preparatory work for the painting *Leda*); Man Ray, sketch, 1940, for the painting *Leda and the Swan*; Betty Dodson, *Leda & the Swan*, 1971-1973 (pencil). | "Body to Body" is based on Bartolomeo Ammannati, *Leda and the Swan,* c. 1536 (marble sculpture, after a lost painting by Michelangelo); Reuben Nakian, *Leda and the Swan*, 1979 (bronze sculpture); Fernando Botero, *Leda y el Cisne*, 1995 (bronze sculpture with black patina).

"Standing Figure," p.64: Henry Moore's *Standing Figure*, 1950, a sculpture, was placed in an outdoor art field, Glenkiln Reservoir, Scotland. The work was stolen in October 2013.

"Art Lessons from Jung's Notebook of Dreams," pp.68-70: This poem references an entirely fictitious, unfinished manuscript that was neither written nor planned by Carl Jung.

Acknowledgements

My thanks to the editors of the following publications in which these poems, sometimes in earlier versions, first appeared:

52/250, A-Minor Magazine, BluePrint Review, Connotation Press, Corium Magazine, The Dead Mule School of Southern Literature, Escape Into Life, Eunoia Review, FRiGG, From East to West, Iodine Poetry Journal, Istanbul Literary Review, > kill author, Lost in Thought, Metazen, MiPOesias, MockingHeart Review, nycBigCityLit, OCHO, Octavo, Olentangy Review, Poets/Artists, Press 1, Spillway, Switched-on Gutenberg, UCity Review, and *Wigleaf*

"Always Comes in Threes" appeared as part of *Poets/Artists* 2014 Fixation Exhibition for the Zhou B Art Center, Chicago, Illinois; "Fragment, with Mask and Horn" received a *Best of the Net* nomination from *BluePrint Review*; "Mountain Verse" received a *Best of the Net* nomination from *The Dead Mule* and also appeared in *The Southern Poetry Anthology*

Cover art: *Clock* by James Owens

Author's photo, Robert Frost's farm: Mary Rasnake